25

essential writing tips

Guide to writing **good** fiction

Alana Woods

ISBN 978-0-9579767-7-1 paperback
ISBN 978-0-9579767-8-8 eBook

Published by WoodsfortheTrees

Website: http://www.alanawoods.com
Email: alanawoods@bigpond.com

First published 2012

Other books by **Alana Woods**

Automaton
Imbroglio
Tapestries and other short stories

Non fiction

Family medical history

What are my credentials for writing this guide, you ask.

For a start my qualifications are a Bachelor of Arts in Professional Writing and a Graduate Diploma in Communication.

I have been a professional editor for over 30 years and have been writing for as many, if not more, years.

My first published novel, *Automaton*, a legal thriller, won the Australian Fast Books Prize in 2003 for best self-published fiction. The judge in his reasoning said *Alana has the enviable ability to keep a reader glued to the pages*. I can't tell you how nice it is to be able to append **Award winning author** to my name forever more. The novel became an Australian best seller.

The reviews I've received for both *Automaton* and my latest thriller *Imbroglio* also mean a lot, coming as they do from readers and authors who don't know me but like the books enough to comment.

Alana Woods

Contents

Introduction

There are many books with advice about writing.

There are thin and thick tomes that focus on how to create books and how to approach publishers, agents, promotion and marketing.

This one focuses on how to improve your writing.

Over the years aspiring authors—writers learning the craft—have asked me to critique their work. Generally, as you would expect, they hope I'm going to say it's wonderful and they shouldn't change a word. I can empathise. I like to think my prose is perfect too.

The fact is that what I see often needs a lot of improvement; I know my initial drafts do.

When I began critiquing I noticed similar weaknesses cropping up in manuscripts and began to formulate a tips sheet for aspiring authors. This guide builds on those tips. I hope they help you as they have others.

Tip 1

The writer's voice

This is the most important part of a story.

Many things contribute to voice and there are as many different voices as there are authors.

I tell aspiring authors that when they have found their own voice they should be wary of suggestions to change it. Publishers can be guilty of this. Just be aware that for everyone who doesn't like your voice there will be others who do. Remember, publishers are people and their opinions are just that, opinions.

What is voice?

It's your writing style; your personality coming through in your writing.

Think about the books you've read that you have really liked. What did you like about them? I bet in large part it was the way the author told the story, perhaps a very easy-to-read style such as Dick Francis, or perhaps the more literary and poetic style of Dorothy Dunnett. I mention these two because although they had very different styles (voices) they are both favourites of mine for the reasons I've mentioned.

So how do you know when you've found your voice? Others can advise on what they think works about your writing but really it's something only you will know. It should fit like a tailor-made suit and you should feel comfortable with it.

Once you've found it, it becomes an integral part of your storytelling.

The tips in this guide all contribute to voice.

For instance, show, don't tell.

Vary how you start sentences.

Vary paragraph and sentence lengths.

When using dialogue remember that:

—it should be real

—it should always further the story

—if combining narrative and dialogue make sure the dialogue goes with the right bit of narrative, otherwise your readers may have a hard time deciding who's saying what.

A pet hate of mine is characters continually using each other's names when conversing. How often do you do it in life? Not often. So limit it to when you think it's necessary.

What about the words you use? Ensure they're the right ones, and don't overuse them.

How do you feel about adverbs? Many years ago they were part of an author's arsenal but overuse them today and your writing will have the ring of an amateur.

Characterisation, too, is important. Your characters need to be part of their world, their time and their social milieu.

And let's not forget story development.

All of these are discussed in the following pages.

But first you must hook the reader.

Tip 2

Hooking the reader

This is known as the literary hook.

It means grabbing the interest of your readers with your opening words. They should be sufficiently intrigued to want to keep reading.

It makes no difference if the reader is a publisher you're trying to interest or someone in a bookstore, real or virtual, looking to buy.

Never forget that if they like the look of your book enough to pick it up and if they actually open it to check out your prose you have seconds to convince them to buy. They will rarely read more than a paragraph or two.

Think of your own book buying habits. Most of us fit the above description.

There is a variety of ways to dangle the hook. In this guide I show you a few.

Action

This is the most popular form of opening because your characters have already hit the ground and are running. I can't think of a better author than Matthew Reilly for this example. Here's the opening to his *Hell Island*:

> Terrified, wounded and now out of ammo, Lieutenant Rick "Razor" Haynes staggered down the tight passageway, blood pouring from a gunshot wound to his left thigh, scratch-marks crisscrossing his face.

Cliff hanger

This is another form of action. Literally or figuratively have someone with their toes hanging over the edge of a location or situation. Say, for example, your lead character wakes up drowning. How you follow it up would be a test of your story-telling skills, yes?

A really off-the-wall statement

This could be something that makes the reader think *What?* What can I think of that is totally outlandish? How about this:

> Life would be good if she wasn't dead.

The quality of your writing

Some readers may be attracted by this rather than the story opening, especially if they're looking for something literary and yours fits the bill. It may, however, limit your readership. It might be better to hook them with the story. Or your talent may encompass both like Dorothy Dunnett. Here's the opening to her *King hereafter*, the story of Macbeth:

> When the year one thousand came, Thorkel Amundason was five years old, and hardly noticed how frightened everyone was.

Dialogue

Some authors believe you need to establish characters before introducing dialogue. But isn't that what dialogue does? Give insight into characters? It's the way I start the story I'm working on at the moment, *Dragline*:

> 'Yes or no?'

Immediately the reader will (I hope) wonder what the question was. They will (again I hope) wonder why the other person is hesitating in answering. And by then I should have hooked them.

Jump in at a crucial moment

This is the way I started my award-winning *Automaton*:

> It wasn't his appearance that unnerved her, unexpected though it was with its neat new track runnelling the middle of his chin, curving through cheek and across the outer corner of his right eye to disappear into the hairline. It wasn't even that they were alike in colouring and delicacy of features.
>
> It was his expression. A mixture of hope and no hope.
>
> He was red-haired, fresh smooth skinned, freckled with a faded tan, 19, and not far from the trial of his life.
>
> For murder.

The device I used was to show the as-yet-unnamed character being unnerved by the appearance of a second character. It poses the question of what has unnerved her. The second paragraph tells you but poses another question: why is his expression a mixture of hope and no hope? The reader needs to keep reading to find out and with any luck by that time they're hooked.

Internalisation

This is how I opened my second novel *Imbroglio*. Something is happening that is causing anxiety.

> The sound entered his ear, swirled through his brain, flowed, eddied around his groin, and sank to his toes. He felt, rather than heard. A mouth touched behind his lobe and trailed to his shoulder and his nerve ends rippled with it. A sense of silk swept across his chest. Coolness licked and a streak of flame ignited his genitals. A major case of elephantiasis. A hand, too small, smoothed and moved. He tensed. The mouth angled over his chest, his stomach and almost ... almost ... frustration exploded.

As the reader you may think you know what's happening. But what are you being told? That this person is feeling rather than hearing, sensing and obviously not seeing. Why? Is he dreaming or is something infinitely more profound occurring? Hopefully you won't be able to resist reading on.

Paint a picture

Describe a scene so evocative or vivid it transports the reader immediately into it or sets the movie in their head rolling. Let's look at Stieg Larsson's *The girl who played with fire*:

> She lay on her back fastened by leather straps to a narrow bed with a steel frame. The harness was tight across her rib cage. Her hands were manacled to the sides of the bed.

I don't know about you but I'm in that room with her already.

Pose a question

This could be an actual question as in *What time of the day is it?* or it could be less obvious, such as *Why the leaves failed to fall that autumn was a question on everyone's lips.*

My advice is to examine the openings of books you like and identify what methods the authors have used to capture your interest.

Whatever device you use it has to raise your readers' curiosity. It has to intrigue, excite, maybe both.

You want your words to leap off the page and immediately imprint a picture in the minds of your readers.

Which leads us to tip 3.

Tip 3

Show, don't tell

This can be frustrating advice because often you are told *don't tell* without an explanation of what *showing* is.

Showing means conjuring images in your readers' minds.

However, it would be a mistake to think that *telling* has no place in writing. It does.

So what's the difference?

Showing conjures images, *telling* gives information.

A reviewer once said my books were like movies playing in his head. He could see, feel and hear what was happening. Another reviewer said she could feel the sun and smell the ocean in *Imbroglio*. Here's an example from *Imbroglio* that I think both may have used as an example because it is descriptive, which is what *showing* is all about:

> The sun had shifted and had her face in a vice, leeching the skin from wet moistureless flesh. Her eyes were swollen, she could barely see, then the sharks came. Circling at first, gauging their prey, accommodating her frantic efforts to get away. The circle was wide and as she wondered if she could swim through the gaps more and more joined the ring until they were tip to tail. Then they began to close the circle, slowly, ritually, and as it tightened they formed two, then three, outer rings. Their fins loomed large the closer they circled. She stopped swimming and watched the fins move in, appalled, fascinated. Like a ballet troupe, as one they altered their course and turned inward. In their rush they grew huge, obliterating the sun, looming like tankers, casting her into black shadows. Then they lunged and she screamed and waited for the pain, rearing waist high clear of the water as they clashed.

Two other ways to *show* is with dialogue and using similes and metaphors, albeit sparingly. See how both contribute to *Automaton* in the following scene:

> She put a hand on his shirt, round about where the ribs come together. Robert looked down at it, bent an elbow, then returned the hand to his side. 'It's been a while since Thierry Richards got under my skin, Robert.' Again he resisted the urge to flatten the fingers against him. Was she telling him not to worry about Richards, in any capacity? His heart pounded. Her fingers increased their pressure and her eyes softened. 'Okay?'
>
> The thought that she was still manipulating fell like a torrent over a cliff and she saw his eyes cloud. Withdrawing everything about herself she stepped back, replaced the glasses and left them to come behind.
>
> He was appalled with himself.

Here, through dialogue, Elisabeth is telling Robert that Thierry is in her past. I could have given an explanation by way of background but that would have been *telling*. Dialogue, as a way of *showing*, is much more powerful. As is a *torrent over a cliff*—a graphic and powerful description of feeling.

Generally speaking, *show* the important elements of your story and use *telling* to move the story along.

Showing is descriptive, *telling* is informative.

Find the balance and you will be on the way to writing a story others will want to read.

Now, let's get on to dialogue.

Tip 4

Dialogue: keep it real

Dialogue brings characters to life.

The skill comes in writing dialogue the way people actually speak, by that I mean keeping your characters true to their world, time and social milieu.

People converse in shorthand. They assume that others understand the context and meaning. The knack to good dialogue is to show this while not losing the sense of what is being said.

Some writers fail to grasp this. They believe they must write complete sentences and be grammatically correct at all times. I agree that narrative must be more disciplined, but not dialogue.

Ask yourself this: do you speak in grammatically correct sentences? Of course you don't. So why should the characters in your stories? Here's an example from *Automaton:*

> 'Phil, it's Robert Murphy. Can you give Joe and me five minutes in, say, twenty?'
>
> 'Yeah, sure,' Detective Sergeant Phillip Milne said, 'What's up?'
>
> 'Tell you when we see you. Where?'
>
> 'You don't want to come in?'
>
> 'I'd prefer not.'
>
> 'Okay. The Wig and Pen?'
>
> 'See you there.'

Do you see what I mean by shorthand? No-one says *police station* but it's obvious that Milne is confirming that Robert and Joe don't want to meet him there.

You can also infer from the conversation that they know each other well enough to speak in such a truncated fashion.

You will have also noticed they're not speaking in grammatically correct or complete sentences. Let's rewrite the conversation so it is correct and complete:

> 'Phil, it's Robert Murphy speaking. Joe and I need to talk to you. Can you spare us five minutes of your time in, say, twenty minutes?'
>
> 'Yeah, sure,' Detective Sergeant Phillip Milne said, 'What's up?'
>
> 'I'll tell you when we see you. Where do you want to meet?'
>
> 'You don't want to come in to the police station?'
>
> 'I'd prefer not.'
>
> 'Okay. Let's meet at the Wig and Pen then?'
>
> 'That will do perfectly. We'll see you there in twenty minutes.'

There's nothing wrong with this. But notice how flat it is. It just doesn't convey what I wanted to convey: urgency, familiarity, and people speaking as they really do.

Adverbs

Let's experiment with the example further. Let's use adverbs to make absolutely sure that readers will understand how the characters are feeling and reacting:

> 'Phil, it's Robert Murphy. Can you give Joe and me five minutes in, say, twenty?' Robert asked imperatively, anxiously.
>
> 'Yeah, sure,' Detective Sergeant Phillip Milne replied warily. 'What's up?'
>
> Robert responded quickly. 'Tell you when we see you. Where?'
>
> 'You don't want to come in?' Milne asked, even more warily.
>
> Robert was cagey. 'I'd prefer not.'
>
> Milne said, sighing, 'Okay. The Wig and Pen?'
>
> Robert said decisively, 'See you there.'

Did the adverbial descriptions add to your understanding? Did the conversation flow more quickly? Or did they intrude on your reading pleasure? I would hazard a guess that your answers would be *no, no* and *yes.*

Adverbs are a thing of the past as far as writing is concerned. That's not to say you should never use them but readers expect their authors to work a bit harder on their descriptions nowadays. Using adverbs is the lazy way and, dare I say it, marks writing as amateurish.

Tip 5

Dialogue: he said, she said

Taking the last tip further, convention recommends generally using *he said, she said* when any dialogue attribution is called for.

This is because other descriptions tend to catch the attention of readers and as an author you don't want that. You want readers to be completely caught up in what your characters are saying.

What are other descriptions? Here's several off the top of my head: *replied, laughed, questioned*. And I'm sure you can think of more.

I'm not advocating never using them. I do. As an example have a look at the excerpt in tip 6 where I use *supplied*. What I'm saying is to think about it before deciding they're needed. In real life you rely on body language and tone to help convey the meaning of your words. When you've finished speaking you don't add, for instance, *I chortled cheerfully* or *Alana sighed regretfully*.

The skill is to get it in to the dialogue itself or the accompanying narrative. Here's a short excerpt from *Imbroglio* to illustrate:

> Noel had her hands in her lap. 'Undesirable? Let me get this straight. You mean he was involved with criminals?'
>
> Nick nodded. 'It isn't general knowledge and I'd like to keep it that way, but Alex did his best to turn us into a money laundering operation from day one. I can't say I was sorry when I heard what happened in Cairns.'
>
> Deal with one shock at a time. 'Money laundering? I thought there were laws to stop that.'

Notice I don't say *Noel said, shocked*. I have internalised the shock Nick's answer has given her.

Tip 6

Dialogue: when three or more characters converse

What if more than two characters are involved in a conversation?

The answer is to be more careful. You don't have to resort to *Alana said, John said* every time if the accompanying narrative and what is being said make it clear who is speaking. Let me give you an example of a three-way exchange in *Imbroglio* in which I attribute only twice:

> The two women said hello. Noel stared at the low-cut strapless freedom of her new acquaintance.
>
> Marion lingered over Noel's name. 'Have we met before?'
>
> Noel opened her mouth.
>
> 'Noel was at the accident scene when Alex Patton died,' William supplied.
>
> Auburn eyebrows rose. 'You knew him? Why was he in Cairns? I never did find that out. You're involved in the company?'
>
> 'No, I work for William.'
>
> 'How did you know Alex then?'
>
> William also seemed interested.
>
> 'I didn't,' Noel said. 'What was he like?'

Notice that I use a mix of narrative and attribution to show who is talking. The narrative furthers the story while I've only used attribution where I thought it necessary to identify the speaker. The attributions are brief so as to not slow the speed of the conversation.

Tip 7

Dialogue: it should carry the story forward

Dialogue has to have a purpose.

In the real world we often speak the most boring and useless of inanities. We pass the time of day saying things that have absolutely no point.

You can't do this in your writing.

Every word, whether it is narrative or dialogue, should be on your page because they need to be there. If they don't, get rid of them. Even those pearls of prose you feel you can't bear to delete; if they don't serve a purpose, cut them. You'll feel better for it afterwards.

As for dialogue, every word should advance the story. It could be shedding light on a situation or character, it could be building tension or suspense or it could be revealing feelings. It can be anything as long as it serves a purpose.

That's not to say that a little bit of passing the time of day isn't at times useful but keep it to a minimum because dialogue needs to have a reason for being. It should help the reader understand more about a character, it should provide information and it should always keep the story moving.

Here's an example from a courtroom scene in *Automaton*:

> Gregory Waite leaned in to the microphone and the judge gave him something else to remember. 'Mr Waite, the microphone is there to record your answers, not amplify your voice. There is no need to lean over it.' The court recording monitor stared expressionlessly at him as, startled, Waite looked for evidence of the equipment. His reactions were familiar to the regulars. This place was a foreign land and its procedures unfathomable customs. The words might be familiar, the language was not.

'I ... er ... I was there for rehabilitation. I'd been in trouble with the police and instead of putting me away they sent me up north.'

'You had broken the law?'

Waite nodded. 'Mm-mm.'

'Mr Waite,' the judge called for his attention, 'you must answer yes or no.'

Gregory Waite's neck twisted as he leaned into the microphone, remembered there was no need, sat up and said, 'Sorry. Yes.'

'What was the nature of your offences?'

He decided it was best to concentrate on the person asking the questions. 'Car theft mostly. A bit of break and enter.'

'And occasioning bodily harm?'

'A couple of times.' It was a hard to decipher mumble.

'Would you repeat that please?'

Loudly and clearly, defiantly, 'A couple of times.'

Strictly speaking the judge's references to the microphone and mumbling are not part of the cross-examination. However, in this instance their purpose is to give an insight into, that is *show*, how Gregory Waite is feeling as he reveals his criminal history.

I like dialogue. If you've read my books you'll know that I use it to build my characters' personalities, thoughts, dreams, feelings and prejudices. Used well with narrative you can build them with nuance so readers feel they are getting to know them as they would a real person, gradually over time.

Tip 8

Dialogue: using names

This is a particular dislike of mine.

How many times do you use a person's name when talking to them? Rarely, I would say. Perhaps on meeting, perhaps on parting, possibly when wanting to make a point and probably when trying to gain their attention.

Listen to conversations around you. Take note of your own and apply what you hear to your writing.

Remember to be sparing. If it sounds awkward, false, or in any other way unnatural, don't use it.

I recently read a book where the author, in every bit of dialogue, had his characters using each other's names every time they conversed. It drove me to exasperation. In fact, it annoyed me so much I couldn't finish it. I have doctored the following conversation from *Imbroglio* for you see what I am talking about:

> Next Noel rang the office. Bridget answered and said William had rung yesterday to say that he and Noel would be taking a few days off. 'Congratulations Noel,' she said.
>
> 'Sorry. What are you talking about, Bridget?'
>
> 'William said you're getting married, Noel.'
>
> 'Oh.'
>
> 'Noel, aren't you?'
>
> She could hear the curiosity. 'Bridget, I can't talk. If William rings again would you ask him to ring the hotel?'
>
> 'What hotel, Noel?'

'He'll know, Bridget. Will you ask him to ring? And Bridget, would you not tell anyone except William that I've rung?' She waited for Bridget to acknowledge. 'Bridget, has someone already asked?'

'Yes Noel. Mr Donaldson, yesterday afternoon and this morning.'

If you think it doesn't sound too bad when read silently, try reading it out loud. It's awful and definitely not how we converse in real life.

Here's the scene as it appears in the book.

Next Noel rang the office. Bridget answered and said that William had rung yesterday to say that he and Noel would be taking a few days off. 'Congratulations,' she said.

'Sorry?'

'William said you're getting married.'

'Oh.'

'Aren't you?'

She could hear the curiosity. 'Bridget, I can't talk. If William rings again would you ask him to ring the hotel?'

'The hotel?'

'He'll know. Will you ask him to ring? And Bridget, would you not tell anyone except William that I've rung?' She waited for Bridget to acknowledge. 'Has someone already asked?'

'Mr Donaldson, yesterday afternoon and again this morning.'

Much better, isn't it. It sounds natural. And notice that there's no need for *he said, she said* when a conversation is under way. It's quite obvious who is saying what.

Tip 9

Dialogue: and paragraph construction

By this I mean making sure dialogue is placed with the right bit of narrative so the reader knows who is speaking. So often I've seen little or no seeming thought go into placement.

Can you tell in this piece from *Imbroglio*:

> Marion herself opened the door, wearing shorts over swimmers. 'I'm out by the pool with the children; we live out there in summer.
>
> 'Come through. We're having iced tea, would you like a glass?'
>
> 'I'd love one,' Noel said, grateful for the cool interior.
>
> 'You have a lovely home.'
>
> 'Thank you.'
>
> Marion said, 'I believe in a place being liveable. What about you?'
>
> 'I have a bed-sit with a balcony. It's bearable for one, impossible for two.' Marion eyed her.
>
> 'You share?' Noel blushed.
>
> 'No.'

That was doctored and perhaps a bit extreme but it makes my point. Now here's the actual version:

> Marion herself opened the door, wearing shorts over swimmers. 'I'm out by the pool with the children; we live out there in summer. Come through. We're having iced tea, would you like a glass?'
>
> 'I'd love one,' Noel said, grateful for the cool interior. 'You have a lovely home.'
>
> 'Thank you,' Marion said, 'I believe in a place being liveable. What about you?'

'I have a bed-sit with a balcony. It's bearable for one, impossible for two.'

Marion eyed her. 'You share?'

Noel blushed. 'No.'

As you can see in the doctored version it doesn't take much to have your reader thinking *Whoa, what?* It's not impossible to work out but why cause them unnecessary difficulty. Your job as a writer is to keep your readers immersed in the story and to do that you need to make sure everything is in its right place.

Enough of dialogue. Let's move on to story structure.

Tip 10

Vary how you start a sentence

When we write a story we want readers to flow smoothly over our words, our phrases, our sentences. For this to happen your writing needs to be fluent. It also needs to avoid monotony.

A most annoying trait to fall into is to repeatedly use the same words to start sentences. Unless, of course, you are using parallelism for effect.

Especially vary the words you begin sentences with in the same paragraph. I notice that writers learning the craft can be guilty of using *The* or a character's name excessively.

Distinctive words

Be careful about opening with words that will stick in your readers' minds.

One that jumps to my mind is *For*. I notice period and fantasy writers use it, I imagine because it conveys a sense of other-worldliness. But it becomes noticeable if used multiple times:

> For it had come to pass …
> For they were not what they seemed …

Can you start with words such as *and, but, because*?

My opinion is that of course you can. Let's be plain, you can start with any word you like as long as it makes sense in the context. You're writing a story, not a treatise on language, and you should use words to their best effect. But as in all things writing, consider, consider, consider before using. Don't stray far from the grammar rules when writing narrative. We discuss this further in Sentence fragments.

Parallelism

Parallelism gives a pattern to a number of sentences that run on from each other. It builds a cadence, a hypnotic quality if you're lucky. It's starting several sentences in the same way and if used well it's very effective.

> What was the reason for Elisabeth's move to Canberra? What was the shock she received on her first day? And what, for heaven's sake, was she up to with Robert?

Tip 11

Mix your sentence lengths

The last thing you want to do as a storyteller is to bore your audience.

A good way to bore is to be monotonous. A good way not to bore is to be interesting. And for storytellers that means using variety.

Variety in the context of this tip means mixing the lengths of your sentences.

Follow a long and perhaps complicated one with something short and snappy, maybe as short as one, two or three words. It adds impact. Here's an example from *Imbroglio*:

> As she sat there under the awning with the sun sheeting the harbour with eye-watering intensity, background noises rose in level, the still hot air acting as an exaggerated conductor. Crockery and cutlery clattered, conversations drifted audibly, children shrilled, someone laughed loudly inside. Noises from the berthed launches were as sharp as if taking place in her eardrum. She looked over at them and let her gaze wander, staring without really seeing one of the berthed cruisers with its subdued hubbub of below deck voices and gentle knocking against the wharf. Stared past the man with the camera propped beside a bollard to which the craft was tied. A seagull wheeled and flung itself past him.
>
> She frowned. His camera seemed to be trained on her. As she looked the man waved, at her she was sure. He stood, lowering the camera. She removed her sunglasses. It was then that Noel received her shock.

Notice that the sentences vary in length but as the tension builds they progressively shorten the closer we come to the shock.

However, I'm not suggesting this is the way you should always lead in to a shock. It's just the way I handled it in this instance.

There will also be times when you will have very good reasons for using a series of long or short sentences.

What I'm trying to impress upon you is to always consciously consider what you want to say and how you want to say it. Always.

Tip 12

Use the right words

Make sure the words you use convey the right thought or meaning.

For example, in one of my novels I typed *phased* instead of *fazed*. It escaped my editor's as well as my attention, made it into the first printed edition of that book and I had to live with it.

Keep a dictionary by your side. Overuse it rather than the opposite.

If you're looking for an alternative word use a thesaurus.

As I have said earlier, the words you choose should fit your characters' world, time and social milieu.

Homophones

Homophones are words with the same pronunciation but different spelling, such as *phased* and *fazed*. Here are some that often confuse:

Affect and *effect*

> How do you think the sale will affect the shares?
> Do you know what effect the sale had on the shares?

Desert and *dessert*

> A desert is a hot and dry place.
> Dessert is my favourite part of a meal.

Currant and *current*

> The currants dried out and went hard.
> The river current was too strong to swim against.

Passed and *past*

> The law was passed by a majority.
> The events of the past influence the future.

Principle and *principal*

> The law is the principle we should all live by.
> The school principal will speak to the class.

Stationary and *stationery*

> The cars were stationary at the starting block.
> The stationery cupboard needs more paper.

The three horrors

There, *their* **and** *they're*

> **There** (a place): We have been invited to go there.
> **Their** (people): We have been invited to their place.
> **They're** (the contracted form of *they are):* They're coming to our place.

I often see *their* misspelt as *thier*. Just remember all three begin with *the*.

Its **and** *It's*

> **Its** (one word): Every good deed receives its reward. (Try using *it's* in this sentence—*it is*—and you'll see it doesn't make sense.)
> **It's** (contraction of *it is* or *it has*): It's (*it is*) going to get very windy later. It's (*it has*) become very windy.

Your **and** *you're*

> **Your** petticoat is showing. (Try using *you're*—*you are*—and you'll see it doesn't make sense.)
> **You're** (contraction of *you are*): You're going to be late.

Honed and *homed*

I'll end the tip with this one because I see *honed* being misused for *homed* time and time again. Apparently it has become common usage in the US but to me it's just wrong.

Hone (to sharpen): The chef honed his knives.
Home (as in to fix on a target): The chef homed in on the dessert.

Tip 13

Don't overuse words

This tip is short and simple.

Try to use different words when describing similar scenes or movement.

A reader contacted me to say he noticed that I had used *alighted* six times, he estimated, in *Imbroglio*. He said he thought it was not overused but because it was not a word he came across often it stood out for him.

I did a global search and found three occurrences. So it must have really made an impression for him to think I had used it more.

What did I replace two of them with? *Got off* and *left*.

What this example illustrates is that it's a good idea to use different words to describe similar things, be they scenes, movement, thoughts or dialogue.

Always keep a dictionary and thesaurus handy.

Tip 14

Spelling, punctuation and grammar

Typographical errors (usually shortened to *typos* or *literals*) in a book give the appearance of its author not being good at their job, which is to tell a story effectively so readers become immersed. They can't do that if they are continually being pulled out of that immersion by errors in spelling, punctuation and grammar.

The more errors your book contains the more you risk losing credibility with your readers.

Misspelt words, especially, mark you out as someone with poor writing skills who has not had their manuscript edited.

Poor punctuation too is a dead giveaway of poor written language skills. I've seen books that look as though the commas have just been shaken randomly over the pages. At best they force the reader to re-read something to understand the meaning. At their worst they completely obfuscate the meaning.

I'll reference here the book by Lynne Truss, *Eats, shoots & leaves: the zero tolerance approach to punctuation*.

Should it be *Eats, shoots and leaves* or *Eats shoots and leaves*.

As you can see, comma placement is crucial.

Grammar forms the rules for constructing language. It determines how you build your sentences, for example tense and first, second or third person consistency. These are discussed in subsequent tips.

If your book contains errors readers will ask themselves why they are bothering with it. They certainly won't bother with your subsequent books.

I say again, use a dictionary and a thesaurus.

Google everything you're unsure of. There's so much advice online that you have no excuse for getting things wrong.

Ask someone who has a good command of the language to check your manuscript. You can't beat other eyes going over your work.

You may think that the publisher who takes you on—because surely one will recognise your genius—will fix those things for you. Think again. Unless you are a genius they're not going to be bothered with a manuscript that needs major work to pull it into shape. Those days are gone.

This is a fact: it's indie (independent, self published) authors who come in for the lion's share of criticism for the quality of their books; the look as well as the text. So do everything in your power to ensure your book doesn't attract this kind of negative attention.

Tip 15

Characterisation

How do you flesh out characters so they are believable and your readers feel they can see, hear and understand them?

Readers must be able to relate to your characters. By novel's end they must care what happens to them if you want them to recommend your book to others. If you doubt this think about your own reading habits and what prompts you to recommend or not recommend a book.

Your characters therefore need to be real, at least within the pages and while your readers are following their story. They need to be three dimensional. They should also not step out of character unless you have a good reason for having them do so.

They should have names that suit them unless, again, you have a good reason for going counter to this, for example the bullying a character received as a child because of their inappropriate name affects their behaviour in the story.

As to a reason for being, even the most minor of characters in your story should only be there if they have a part to play.

What does all of this tell you?

It should tell you that you, the author, must know your characters before you write them into existence.

Character development

Resist giving a full description of your characters: their looks, their family history, where they work and everything else about them the moment you introduce them to your readers.

To begin give only what is needed, then fill them in over the following chapters.

Think of when you meet new friends or work colleagues. You notice some things about them immediately but others only become apparent as you get to know them. I'm talking about such things as the depths of their character, idiosyncrasies and foibles, likes and dislikes, irritating or endearing habits, strengths and weaknesses, what drives them, the kind of clothes they like to wear and the cars they drive. Generally it happens slowly.

There may be times when you take an instant dislike to someone and this is reinforced or reversed the more you get to know them.

Keep in mind your goal for your characters. Are they going to appear to be the good guy or the bad guy and is this going to be apparent immediately or is it going to come as a surprise? Or is the like or dislike going to build slowly with subtle hints?

Character description

Think about how much detail you put into your characters' physical descriptions. Do you need everything including ring sizes and the number of freckles on noses? Or would broad brushstrokes and letting readers form their own images be better?

It's up to you but I suggest this. Think about your favourite books. How did those authors tackle character description? If you can't remember then re-read them and take note.

Let me also set you an exercise. Pick a fictional character from a book that you know well and others in your circle know well. Ask them which actor would best represent that character. I'd hazard a guess that not everyone would suggest the same actor.

Why? Because everyone forms their own mind picture of what a character in a book looks like.

Here's another exercise. Ask your circle—individually so they don't influence each other—to describe a person who is not present. If they answer with nondescript descriptions such as brown eyes and a bit chubby, ask them to tell you something that would make spotting the person in a crowd possible. That's the sort of thing you're after when developing characters: the things that make them who they are.

What do I mean by that? Well, perhaps someone is unusually tall and thin and they hunch their shoulders in an attempt not to stand out. Perhaps someone has long hair that they never tie back, so it's always falling over their face. Then again, maybe you don't want them to have anything that is unique, maybe you want them to blend into the background.

The saying *less is more* springs to mind. Lengthy description can prompt readers to skim or skip and that's the last thing you want because it's going to influence what they say about your book to others.

My final word on this is that it's up to you.

But I will repeat: consider, consider, consider.

Tip 16

Story development

Now let's look at how you develop your story.

Stories all have a beginning, a middle and an end.

The beginning hooks the reader and sets the scene.

The middle tells the story.

The end brings about a resolution or closes the story.

A typical novel is around 80,000 to 150,000 words long. It may contain a host of characters and take the reader on a long journey in time, travel or events. Some authors plan their story first while others write by the seat of their pants.

Whatever way you prefer to tackle yours there are some decisions you'll need to make before starting. These are whether to use 1st/2nd/3rd person point of view, single or multiple points of view and tense.

When writing you will need to be ever vigilant about active voice versus passive voice, sentence fragments and excessive description.

I'm going to break these into separate tips because there is a lot to cover.

Tip 17

Story development: 1st/2nd/3rd person points of view (POV)

This is the perspective from which your story is told.

First person means telling the story from one character's point of view. You use *I*, *me*, *we*. You are limited to telling only what that character knows. An example is Daphne Du Maurier's *Rebecca*. If you haven't read it I recommend it. This is its wonderfully evocative opening:

> Last night I dreamt I went to Manderley again.

Second person is not often used, perhaps because it is the most difficult to sustain. It's used more in short stories than novels. The *You* form is used. It's very intimate. It's as though you are telling yourself the story. Again, as a writer it restricts you to a single point of view.

I refer you to Morgen Bailey who has written a number of short stories in second person. Here's the beginning to one:

> You struggle to breathe as you look down at the cot. You know he won't be far away. It's only a matter of time.
>
> Your heart quickens as you hear gravel shifting. A large car – his Daimler. You've got it all planned but of course there's no guarantee ... What if ...? It's no good thinking what if? you tell yourself. You only have one chance. To escape. Be free. Alive again. You stand up straight and your hands tighten around the bundle you hold close to your chest. It's the key to everything. This is what it's come to, you know he's here to kill you, take your child, his heir.

If you'd like to read more about second person point of view Morgen's blogspot is at http://morgenbailey.wordpress.com/2ppov/.

You may also like to check out her second person *Tuesday tales* page at http://morgenbailey.wordpress.com/tuesday-tales/.

Third person is what the majority of writers use. You use *he, she, him, her, they, them.*

Third person **omniscient** allows the storyteller to know and reveal the thoughts, feelings and actions of all characters in the story.

Both *Automaton* and *Imbroglio*, my suspense thrillers, are written in third person omniscient point of view.

Third person **limited** (also known as third person intimate) allows the reader to know only the thoughts and feelings of a single character. It differs from first person in that it is the author's voice, not the character's voice, that you hear. JK Rowling's *Harry Potter* series is an example. Readers only ever know what Harry knows.

Tip 18

Story development: single or multiple points of view

Another aspect of point of view is deciding whether to follow one or multiple characters. Following one throughout is the most common.

If you choose to follow multiple characters be careful because frequent and quick changes may confuse your readers.

With multiples the changes are best done at chapter breaks. But if you want to move between characters within one chapter do it at breaks in the narrative—those extra line spaces between paragraphs which indicate such things as a break in sequence, a time lapse or a change of location. These breaks are alerts to your readers that a change of some sort is about to happen.

Automaton and *Imbroglio* both follow two characters. Here's an example from *Imbroglio* in which I change points of view within a chapter and indicate it with larger than normal spacing between paragraphs:

'Australians all let us rejoice, for——' Forgetting to move her feet a wave slapped into Noel's mouth and she sank. Coming up spluttering she flung 'Thank you' to the impartial guide and drew her extended hands together to begin the long swim home.

He had had all day but Browning had not yet picked up David's mother. David was worried. Browning had said he would wait for her himself. She had to put in an appearance at some stage.

Noel's arms were tired and her neck stiff from holding her mouth above water. At first she had tried breaststroking normally, submerging with every pull, but her eyes had begun to sting, her hair clung to her face, and the forced breathing took its toll.

Tip 19

Story development: tense

I'm not going to get into the intricacies of tense (past, present and future continuous and perfect) because if you're adept enough with the language to be writing or contemplating writing a novel then you will be using them probably without knowing.

Just remember there is past, present and future and ensure you don't inadvertently slip between them.

Past tense: She fed the horse this morning.
Present tense: She is feeding the horse now.
Future tense: She will feed the horse shortly.

In a novel length story all three can be employed. The main one is usually present tense, but if you use flashback and/or projection then you will also use past and future. If you are going to switch, make it obvious so you don't confuse your readers.

Tip 20

Story development: active and passive voices

What are these? Let me give you some examples.

Active: The chef honed the knife.
Passive: The knife was honed by the chef.

Active: Noel put the letter down.
Passive: The letter was put down by Noel.

Active voice shows the subject performing the action. Active is live action, passive is not.

In active voice the subject comes first in the sentence.

Which one has more impact? Active of course. So be vigilant. Don't fall into passive unless you're using it for a reason.

Tip 21

Story development: excessive description

We touched on this in character description.

If you like the classics you'll know those authors could go into great detail when describing locations, characters and scenery. Those were more leisurely times. The modern reader is generally impatient with excessive description and may well skim or skip. I know I do. I read a story not long ago that described the various states of love for the length of several pages. I read the first two paragraphs, became impatient and flipped through the pages to find where the story took over again.

For the modern author the skill comes in painting a picture succinctly.

Tip 22

Story development: sentence fragments

These are incomplete sentences and some people get hung up about their use, more so in narrative than in dialogue.

My advice is this: if you know the rules then you will know when you can get away with breaking them. (If you don't know the rules consider taking a remedial language course.)

If sentence fragments make sense in the context, use them. They can be incredibly effective. Don't know what they are? Here's an example:

> She hoped the Montgomery's were sleeping. And Russell.

This is taken from *Automaton*. I could have written it several ways, for example:

> She hoped the Montgomery's and Russell were sleeping.
>
> She hoped the Montgomery's were sleeping. She hoped Russell was sleeping too.

In the story context I was conveying a mood, a thought that was continuing. And the fragment—*And Russell.*—expressed it best.

A complete sentence contains a subject and a predicate (that is, a verb, the action). The above example does not. It contains only the subject.

Tip 23

Story development: the ending

Tip 2 discussed the importance of the beginning of a story, that you must have a hook to keep your readers reading.

The tips that followed were about making the middle of your story compelling.

So we should finish by looking briefly at endings.

As with everything about writing there are no hard and fast rules about how to end stories. Aim for impact is the advice you'll generally receive.

It could be a wedding, an arrest or the baddie getting killed. It could be your characters riding or sailing off into the sunset and your readers figuratively going with them.

We've all heard people say *I couldn't get that story out of my head for days.* That's what you should aim for.

Tip 24

When the story is written

Put your manuscript away for a while—I put mine away for a year or longer—so that when you return to it the story is fresh again in your mind.

When you're ready to get back to it print out a copy. It's much more effective looking at the printed page when you're checking for errors.

Read everything, and I mean everything, aloud—even your 100,000 word novels—from beginning to end.

Read it as though you're reading to an audience, with all the pauses and inflections. Misplaced punctuation in particular will jump out at you.

You don't have to do it all in one hit. In fact you shouldn't, because after a while you stop listening to yourself.

Reading aloud is essential to find, for example those missing words that your brain has *inserted* when reading.

It is essential to hear what sounds awkward and unreal.

Another trick authors use to try to catch their mistakes is to check the manuscript backwards, sentence by sentence.

I use a ruler. It forces my eye to stay on the line I'm checking.

There is also the one-on-one proofread. This is where two people sit together, both with a copy of the manuscript in front of them. One reads the story aloud, including capitals, punctuation etc., and the other person checks what is being read against their copy. Both use rulers. This is an almost foolproof method for picking up errors.

However, no amount of self-editing and proofreading beats having a professional editor go over it for you. If you hire them to do a copy edit they won't only be checking for errors, they'll be looking for ways that you can improve your story.

Having said that, if you want to take the risk of not engaging an editor, by using the self-editing suggestions you should at least have a reasonably, if not fully, mistake-free manuscript.

At the risk of labouring the point I will finish the tip with this: The mantra of professional editors is *Never ever edit your own work*. You are too close to it and you miss too much.

Tip 25

Wrapping up

This guide is a foundation upon which to build your writing talents.

If you follow these tips I can't guarantee that you will become a best selling author but your writing should improve.

To finish I urge you, once you are happy with your story and have had it edited, to make it look as good as it reads.

The next step is to have it professionally formatted. You may well be able to do this yourself. But, again, don't settle for less than best.

Finally the cover. Don't compromise. It pays to have one professionally produced.

Remember, your book must look at least as good as all the others on the shelves in the real and virtual bookstores. If possible it should stand out so it attracts attention.

Now you know my tips I invite you to buy and read my books. And by all means get back to me and tell me if you think I follow my own advice.

A last word

As you dip your toes into the world of being a published author you'll realise that reviews of your books are important and you'll spend some of your marketing and promotion time chasing them.

On that score I wonder if you would be kind enough to leave a review of this guide on Amazon, and Goodreads if you are a member (if you're not, as an author you should be).

You may also like to post it on my website: http//www.alanawoods.com and anywhere else you wish.

And if you read *Automaton* and *Imbroglio* reviews of them would also be very appreciated.

I look forward to catching up with you in the various forums.